In Her Light

Also by Christi Steyn

What the Moon Gave Her

In Her Light

christi steyn

Andrews McMeel
PUBLISHING®

Andrews McMeel Publishing
a division of Andrews McMeel Universal
1130 Walnut Street, Kansas City, Missouri 64106

www.andrewsmcmeel.com

24 25 26 27 28 VEP 10 9 8 7 6 5 4 3 2 1

ISBN: 978-1-5248-9475-7

Library of Congress Control Number: 2024940548

Editor: Patty Rice
Art Director: Julie Barnes
Production Editor: Elizabeth A. Garcia
Production Manager: Chuck Harper

Illustrations by Justin Estcourt

for the ones who dance the hardest,
cry like fountains,
and love without limits

never change a thing

chapters

author's note

Hello there, person with a new book. It's always exciting to start something new. I hope these poems add light to your day. I have endless wishes for you. The first wish is a big one: falling head over heels with life itself. Yep, even the tricky bits—because, let's face it, the hard parts are responsible for your growth.

There are all kinds of poems in here. Find the ones that speak to your heart. The firefly poems are for times of uncertainty. It's okay to be a little lost; I've been there, too, but you'll come to find there is always a path leading you to a space of calm. *A guide in times of darkness when you feel alone.* I have this gift: I enjoy my own company a lot, and my favourite people are the ones with whom silence is comfortable. I love it. You'll write, I'll read, you'll doodle, I'll ponder the mysteries of the universe. Friendships are wonderful when they can recharge your soul. Let this book be that friend to you.

Poetry always shows up for me at just the right moment. There are different styles and poems that don't always make sense right away, but perhaps there is a line that stays in your memory. It's all about the moments that stick—whatever you need to hear, simply underline it. Glitter, highlight, and illustrate as much as you want. I will leave a few blank pages at the back of this book for your own scribbles and musings. My favourite pastime is reading poems with a pen in my hand and jotting down thoughts as they come. Let my poems be a doorway for your creativity.

I describe myself as a sensitive soul who tries to cultivate dragon-like traits: little roars and fire-breathing classes each day to develop more courage. I do this by writing down my needs, desires, and where I want to be. I don't want to revert back into a tiny-me where life screams in my direction. I am only honest, or I try to be. When the small feelings grow in my heart, I know that I have to snap out of it. Remember, the light always comes back. Be patient; the fireflies will kiss you, and life will be sweet once again. *Hold on, friend.*

chapter one

Return of the Fireflies

searching for light

this goes out to the sensitive soul
the one whose emotions can take control
to the loner who isn't physically alone
and always carries a heart of gold
to the one who is kind yet somehow feels left behind
to the one who has time, who listens
who attends with an eye that glistens
to the one who never walks away
to the one who hurts but always stays
this goes out to the one who is lost but remains soft
the one who loves with their fingers crossed
the one who wishes to be understood
who was treated poorly but remains good
to the one who isn't lucky, who almost gave in
this is not your ending but where you begin

if you lost a piece of yourself that you love,
make a promise to search for it again

the anatomy of light

hello, firefly, it's okay if you forgot how to shine today
the world can be a bit exhausting at times

fireflies don't always need to glow
you can recharge
you can rest
you will have your moment in the sun

it's okay to feel lost
be open to all your feelings
in time, you will come out of hiding
and, oh baby, you'll be shining

star

we are all born from darkness
it is the only way to know light
if you grow up afraid of the dark,
you can burn a candle and wait,
but don't forget, you know it well
you are born from darkness
do not be afraid
the other side will soon return
you are made with fire
far greater than any fear
do not run from the dark
for you are strong, right here

we love to have you near

the sky is not always clear
people are not always dear
but there is no end, we extend past death
consumed by breath
how wonderful this living
a dance worth whirling
worth slurping
oh, look, a brand-new day
stay
a better time will soon appear
the world is lucky to have you here

the witch in your gut

if you always do what is expected,
or perfect, or acceptable,
you will lose all your fire
you must shake it awake before it turns to ash
there are dragons swimming through your veins
you can't settle for being tamed
you have no idea how powerful you are
and yet, here you stand, eager to please
for what? listen to the witch in your gut
the one you've been told to hide down deep
the one who emerges every time you sleep
see,
you are capable of so much more
you're restless
'cause the lion inside
is desperate to roar

let it sink in

you are not hard to love
when someone tells you
you are beautiful,
they mean it
when they tell you
you are captivating,
you don't have wonder whether you deserve it or not
all the words are meant for you, you are not a burden
you are worth the world

poem for the sun

the sun is happy to see me today
finally
he has been away for a long time
i felt neglected and lost my confidence,
   telling myself a story
maybe i do not deserve the warmth
but here he rises and greets me like an old friend
   once again
it's good to see you
i missed you
don't be scarce
i need you

how to find yourself

you are searching to find yourself,
but you will never find yourself completely
and to be honest
how boring would that be?
you will, however, find glimpses of your soul
and see that, when you are shattered,
you are still whole
you will find yourself on a trampoline
high and low and in-between
you will see yourself
in a kaleidoscope
you will call her Hope
you will see pieces of yourself in every day
speak with kindness when choosing what to say
you can stare at the moon and yell, "that's me!"
when you feel lost, you must go to the sea
you will never find yourself completely
in a messy life, with a contrast of dark and bright
there is more to you than i ever could write

oh, to be like the ones

i want to be like the ones who recite crystals and stars
the ones who have scars
i want the ones self-assured
happy when they're bored
i want the ones who love horses, who braid flowers
  in their hair
the ones who dance like air
they care and always hug a little longer
they carry eyes of wonder
naming trees, thanking bees
when life is heavy, they release
and stay young for the rest of their lives
for this life is paradise
seeing and feeling beauty is how we survive

time will tell

it is scary when you stop finding joy in things you
  used to love
you might need time
it is not necessary to rush towards what you expect
  from yourself
be gentle
it takes courage to be gentle
keep on carrying the hope
your happiness will always return

exist entirely

don't apologise for the space you take
like the ocean and her waves
how cruel if she were to be small?
only a puddle with drops that crawl
grow
and grow more
don't live like a corpse
the world needs all of you
the true self is a grand view
judgement is something to unclothe
only then can you experience growth

if you have anxiety

i won't tell you not to have it
or to think of something else
it does exist
how i have breathed panic and felt like a fraud
one cannot simply relax or wish it away
it does exist, and when you find yourself
  lost and anxious,
separated from your body,
i invite you to come back,
back to yourself
stay in the discomfort
do not run away, simply listen to what your body
  is telling you
be still and feel
we cannot hide from ourselves
anxiety is telling you something
listen

come back to who you are

what would happen if you stopped trying to change
and instead came closer to who you already are?
what would happen then?
when you do more for yourself and less to impress,
the world is happening from you
and for you
come closer to who you are
do not wait for an arrival
you have arrived

it's another day

you are in this moment for the first time
  and the last time
it is not simply another day
it is an invitation to be here
to stop living in the future and in tomorrow
no more daydreaming away from yourself
bring it back
it's not just another day
you are here to experience all life has to offer
be mindful, breathe, feel
it's another day
you are living
and that is all you need

you are the firefly

when darkness comes,
we can feel stuck, with nowhere to run,
but there is a light switch within
that whispers *begin*

under the covers of a sunken bed
of a day that will end
there is a home where you can return,
where the firefly, once again, will burn

look for the shine, the light to remind
all shadows fade and dissolve
you evolve,
you find a light, you fly

and fall?
sometimes
you learn to yearn for the life of fireflies
and, like the sun, you always rise

in the chaos, we float on clouds

close your eyes
pretend you are on a cloud
it is warm and soft and safe
rest here
let the outside world melt away
just here with yourself
take a moment, brew the tea
rub your hands together
return to the cloud when need be

from hands to wings

i cannot keep waiting for fireflies to arrive
the window is open, but winter is my only guest
where do i find the spark of life?
it's as if i have been drifting in water
candles cannot burn on these fingertips
there is a hole that won't fill
i started drawing my fireflies on paper
let them grow in my mind
music will play
if i make my own light
i hope the fireflies stay

you

you are not too much,
you are not too sensitive,
too loud, too intense, too extra, too silly
you are the level of crazy that i like
the world is lucky to have you

self-heal

you compliment all your friends
every size and smile, they have no faults in your eyes
they can do little wrong,
but the moment you look in the mirror,
you only focus on things you wish to change
have you ever given yourself a compliment?
or do you punish yourself because the world never
  taught you
how to be anything other than perfect?

let me introduce you to the storm
that lives inside your body

maybe, just maybe, if you can look at yourself
  with wonder

and meet that inner thunder,
self-admiration will grow
the garden in your mind will blossom
turn your spark on
the lightning is there, all over your eyes
how it blinds
you weren't born for the norm
remember, you are the storm

i spy with my butterfly eyes

you are the universe
experiencing itself
over and over again
look through the eyes of the world
do you see it?
do you see how magnificent you are?

**there is a whole world out there,
and you are thinking about yesterday**

today is the perfect day to forgive yourself
for all the goals you have not yet achieved
and the dreams that, for the moment, you had to leave
you have not failed, you have given yourself space
and embraced uncertainty
life is filled with possibility
we have now and the future, and perhaps
today is the perfect day to stop beating yourself up
you can always refill your cup
and start again, my friend
unlock the gates
come, a world awaits

you are stronger than the shadows

what if you wash away your insignificance?
climb mountains and howl off into the distance?
be the wolf in your fairy story
wear the moon, cloaked in glory

the shadows will come
let them feast
you will grow again, a phoenix,
a gorgeous beast
the shadows can try and, oh, will they try
they seem to forget

you are with the sky

i invite you to welcome the quiet back into your life
in a world where we are programmed to love the rush,
sit back and invite the calm
use your time to dive into something you love
allow yourself to disappear
read, paint, draw, walk with your
eyes, and take in the air
stare at a rose, the detail will surprise you
do not chase the trap of instant gratification
find the treasure
turn the music on and dance
no more half-living, we savour it all

escape

hello, restless soul
how far you dance into corners to be alone

being lost is not insanity
it feels that way
as long as you don't lose yourself,
you won't stray

never turn yourself into less
find your way through a tangled mess

and keep speaking your own tongue
your heart and lungs
dance to the corners and get lost,
your world can stand, your world can watch

the truth about light

i understand light
i've always understood light,
have not always felt the light
i know the light, need the light,
cannot be the light
pray for it on days it dances away
soon the light will come, and i will greet it
soon the light will come, and i will be it
for now, i am drenched in darkness,
the moon as my cocoon as she whispers,
kissing blisters
you need rest, don't force the light
quiet the lamps, you need more night

dragon high

not everyone is rooting for me
because i am *terrifying*
walking against a flood
so long it took to be accepted and loved

i woke and saw perfection doesn't exist
i am here like a crisis
my own storm as i drown
no one invited to calm me down
let me swallow the night
give me dragons to bite
i hate your approval, it does nothing for me
prefer to be surrounded by truth and the sea
myself, myself, and those that don't fear
i am not here for you
living for fake smiles has never been true
i want the real, and the feeling, and the
    "what is the meaning?"
i cannot be everyone's cup of tea
build the life you want, not something to show
no competition with people you know
live for yourself, look deep, and find desire
don't please the crowds, and take yourself higher

inner child

i am sorry we had to grow up so fast
maybe we can be kids a bit longer?
will you dance in poetry with me?
make rhymes and climb a maple tree?
we can dress like summer,
we can sing in colour
dribble wet sand for wobbly ocean towers
paint faces like flowers
let's make the world beautiful
me and you, a little team
create a life we saw *once upon a dream*
i write every poem with you by my side
you see, these words are where we collide
i love you, you're never far
in the dark, you are my glowing star
we are forever on pages, performing on stages
let me hold you tight
get closer
you bring the light

love poem to darkness

i love the dark
how necessary it is
we all need it to sleep and rest
the quiet is my favourite guest,
and when the night descends to its deepest hue,
the stars unveil their brightest view

wild one

if they don't like you, i'm sure they have terrible taste,
but not everyone is going to like you
it means you're doing something right
keep showing up as yourself, don't please the crowds,
don't wear what everyone is wearing,
don't be quiet when people are rude or wrong
life's too short not to stand up for yourself
there's enough of everyone else
don't drown in normality
you have no immortality
be wild, be bright, be brave
and for the love of all things,
don't behave

shine your light away

stop explaining your art to people who won't
  understand your magic
let them sleepwalk through life
let them keep their advice and their meetings
be selective in your surrendering
being vulnerable is a gift to give
let people leave
you have nothing to lose
they can follow if they choose
ignore the questions, the conversation rejections
you are a poet, an artist, a miracle
let them look at you without knowing your life
being different is divine
take the judgement, you'll be just fine

phoenix

i care more for the person who i am yet to be
the old version does not define me
with each day, i grow
i'm not the girl you used to know
i have learned
been burned
but risen, anew
this life i choose
don't wallow in days that are already gone
look for the person you'll soon become

chapter two

With My Heart on My Sleeve

i was never your poem,
but you were every single one of mine

the heart who spoke for the first time

now that heart has a voice,
heart is excited to speak
heart will confess her love every day
heart is very fond of you
absolute crazy butterflies all bumping into each other
  on the inside
no one can catch them
heart is alive!
now that heart has a voice,
heart won't ever stop saying your name
heart loves your name
heart doesn't want you to leave
heart was made to love and only wants to love
heart will annoy you with too much love
oh, i see
heart can be too much
heart thinks about forever and sees only your face
when you are mad, heart feels sadness in a big, bad way

heart thinks this is unfair
why is a lot of love also a lot of sadness?
heart has questions
questions don't mean answers
heart wishes to feel a little less, please?
when heart tries to love less
heart breaks, it stings
heart wishes to be a bit smaller
heart only wants to be held
no one is listening
heart doesn't want a voice anymore
voice only gets heart in trouble
why does heart love more than other hearts?
from today, heart no longer speaks
it's much safer to stick to heart's beats

kissing shadows

i've met with your shadows, and i don't mind them
we all learn to dance with devils somewhere along
  the way to heaven
you're not a fallen angel, but everything about you
  feels holy
even the parts you cast away, i'll take it
i'll kiss your insecurities 'til you're naked
your love could never hurt me
not when you're the one i prayed for when i was young
someone must have listened
maybe i'll meet them one day
i see it as the trees wink at me, the universe knows
  something

they know i need your light
from sun to midnight
as we grow towards each other like flowers finding
  their hands,
don't fall over, i'll help you stand
hush, i'm right here, simply ask
our love can be slow, but my heart
my heart is *fast*

when you forget how to stop crying

i will take your pain and build a large boat
i want to make a home for your sadness
one with a welcome mat,
heated blankets and a porcelain statue of two
  turtles hugging

allow me to care
there's nothing broken you cannot share
the bed is made
the plumber paid

your grief is no burden to hide
i'll carry the darkness
let me stay by your side

i've always wanted to be someone's dream girl

he'd look at me and love to hear about my day
someone excited to spend time, who wants me to stay
i wish i had more confidence,
that i could feel interesting and beautiful and captivating
it's a strange feeling when you realise
you should probably love yourself a bit more
when you see how much you judge, and it's made
  you insecure
it's hard to be invisible with no strength to be seen
maybe, one day, he'll be more than just a silly dream

growing pains

i am a woman,
but i sometimes feel like a girl
questioning my place in this big world
i don't always know where i belong
some days it's quite tough to be certain and strong
my path can seem blurry and often unsure
with many successful people, i can't help but keep score
everyone appears to have it all figured out
i'm trying to understand what i'm crying about
there's this fear i'm doing it all wrong
like some different path i should follow along
people only show when it's going well
when things are bad, they'd rather not tell
no one spends their life entirely in the sun
so if you're struggling, you're not the only one

this heartbeat is too loud

my greatest fear is losing you
how i would miss stealing socks from your cupboard
and hearing your laugh
i would miss the way you hold a towel for me
  after a swim
i love scratching your neck and seeing you flop forward
this i will miss
each touch, how it seems so thoughtful
how you put on my seat belt
making food together
saying this is *forever*
i am scared to lose what we have become
this simply proves our love isn't done

perhaps it's your turn to start disappointing some people,
especially if you have disappointed yourself enough

you are not one to waste love

have you ever known someone was going
  to break your heart?
you knew but kept pretending nothing was wrong
hoping they would stay because you had so much
  love to give
and if they left, you wouldn't have any place to put it
you don't want to throw all that love away
and when your worst fear came true,
it all happened in slow motion
you were out of your body,
only a spectator viewing a nightmare
if only you could go back in time
and stop yourself from ever falling in the first place
maybe all that love would be better off somewhere else

love me in colour
make it loud
if a tree falls in a forest,
let there be sound

the girl who wishes for wings

her eyes are starry skies
she sucks at goodbyes
prefers to leave without a word
if she could, she'd be a bird

the wind knows her name
they're one and the same
she's lost but never alone
her heart is her home

if she could, she'd live all around
where she goes, she's always found

missing sunshine gloves

i tried catching sunshine in the pockets
  of my favourite dress
the light kept slipping out
now my hands are always cold,
and your hands are too far,

too far to hold

half a heart

you gave me the promise of your heart,
and i built a box for safekeeping,
decorating every inch with lipstick kisses
  and poems of forever
i took my job seriously, "not a scratch," i said
and because you trusted me with your precious heart,
i gave you mine in return,
but you never had a box to place it in
you kept it in your hands, left it on the subway,
  scratched the outside,
and when you got tired of carrying the extra weight,
you gave it back
and when you gave it to me, i could not recognise
  my own heart
is it still mine?

a sight for sore eyes

he is beautiful
easy on the eyes
easy
easy heart
not so fast
he does not belong to you
the wind can take him away again
heaven on earth does not exist in his arms
it will feel that way
he feels like your entire world
he can't be the most important thing in your life
but, boy, he surely is a sight for sore eyes

i don't want you waiting around for anyone

don't wait for them to call
focus on your own life
don't settle for someone who doesn't make you feel good
if they treat you wrong,
move on
and don't wait for an apology
don't obsess and check constantly
there is too much living you are missing
don't wait for them to realise you're the one
there will be someone who wouldn't dare let you go
they would never make that mistake
don't sit on your knees and plead to be saved
it's too late, don't settle for less
don't stay if they make you guess
love should be obvious and safe and sweet
you don't need them
you are complete

it's a bad day, not a forever day

i can't explain why i am not well
trying to rationalise the pain and the numb
by morning it had begun, googling *how to be human*
but i cannot find the sun, i know how to drown
it won't help, my instincts are not fixing things
i am not well, like the stories i repeatedly tell,
like if i cry louder, perhaps you will hear me and reach out,
like if my tears fall for longer periods of time,
perhaps you will feel your heart as mine
these methods don't work
i don't like to smoke, but i wish to be filled with fog
i have been trying to get better, and people want
  me to explain,
to speak, there is no tongue in a body this weak
go ahead and try, there is more to light than saying "sky"
therefore, i collapse into myself
and conjure every ounce of help

your hands are burning from holding on

if they don't show you that they care,
it might be time to look after yourself
you are used to putting others first
seeing them shine makes you happy,
but when you find yourself empty,
it might be time to let go

my own world

you were such a beautiful thing in my mind,
  and i only ever loved you
yes, i know i was the one to leave, but you were
  no good to me
the world wasn't mine anymore
it was your world with me in it
do you understand?
i won't accept a love like that anymore
i need to create a world for myself

thinking about a younger time

have you seen how i disappear in gardens?
picking the leaves and running around

jumping on trampolines, saving insects from near death
  by swimming pool
hours of time alone, climbing trees, calling them home
you must understand how little i spoke
bubbles in the bath with hands of soap
"she keeps herself busy, how sweet"
have you noticed the girl can't speak?
silent at the dinner table
dreaming in drawings
"she'll be fine, she'll teach herself how to write"
no one knows she's scared every night
her mind goes wild with make-believe, now she doesn't
  trust her trees
she has herself and a bedside lamp
wishing to be held and maybe heard
believes she'll learn to talk to birds
the girl grew up and was able to see
her childhood was always her poetry

a letter to loneliness

hello, loneliness, i am writing this letter to check in
you are standing between other words already
do you feel lonely between others?
why does being alone make me feel like a failure?
why do i crave you but go blank when you arrive?
do you know hurt without bruises?
how much do we have in common?
are you my synonym? i think about you a lot
do you feel loved when people think of you?
does love ever scare you as much as it scares me?
do you love me?
we spend so much time together,
and i don't know if you like your name
where do you live? in books? on mountains? in my poetry?
do you know what a hand feels like?
do you live in my hand when i place it on my chest?
tell me, where do you rest? what i really want to ask is,
"when will you become my friend?"
is it an enemies-to-lovers sort of trope?
if i say, "i love loneliness," will it come true?
what i really want to know is
am i you?

will you learn to love me?

most days, i believe, if it weren't for me,
we wouldn't resolve things
it is my job to call after a fight,
to teach talking
i listen for glass in your voice
and pick it up before it cuts
say, "i love you," no matter what
i love more and better,
and then i wait for you to do the same
some days i see it, as i live for glimpses
if it weren't for me
i don't think we'd be
it's exhausting to love this hard
i can't force you to respond
and learn to love me like i love you
but, baby, with my heart
i wish you had a clue

sky-crossed lovers

you are a cloud
i am the sky
you only visit at times
when you are gone, i look for the sun,
but he is loved by everyone
your shape started to change,
but i loved you in all your ways

when it is dark, you're harder to spot
even when i am always here
your crystal drops will disappear
my colours are different shades of blue
because i'll never heal
from losing you

you don't know what a moon is

i introduced you to the moon that lives inside of me,
and you held her tightly
how naive to think you were hugging me close
as you forced the moon to explode
but, darling, this moon is not made of plastic
this is no balloon or cheese,
not something to squeeze like fragile bone
she is made of stone, of gold
close your eyes, don't see her shine
never forget, this moon is mine

everyone wants to love a poet, but . . .

what about the days when i forget everything
except that i love you?
what happens when i don't feel loved back?
where does one put away worries and dread?
why does it not sink in (the words i've said)?
i pick flowers to see your face in the centre
i light candles and imagine your touch, tender
i feel sick and weak, it's easier to bleed
being pulled from within, nothing but touch to cure skin
i hate how much i want to become,
hate how i ache to always be one,
looking like a person, this head attached to a body,
living like a ghost, softly sobbing
if you knew how i was, you would leave quite soon
you tried to be poetic and called me *your moon*
i believe you're trying to understand
this i know by your eyes and hand,
the way i am held, your spell
the dream is to love a poet, 'til you find we are nothing
  but wrecked
wanting to be loved is the darkest secret i've kept

uncommon superpowers

trust me, i want to wish the bad away
there isn't a day i don't want to smother you
with warm hugs and ear-to-eyebrow kisses
i want to build a bed to personify the word "safety"
a place where promises still mean something,
where humans will realise how unhappy selfishness
  will make them
i want to give away the cure for hate or power or envy
i don't know the difference anymore
i've always tried to surround myself with good
how ignorant to think humans could be understood

my grandmother used to give swimming lessons

we were at the beach when she died
i was 12, and my mother wore sunglasses
  after the sun was
long gone, and i felt confused
i didn't know mothers could cry like that, and
no one ever told me mothers were allowed to die
i suggested role-play: "let me be your mother now"
"i'd like that," she said
we ran to the ocean, straight to the birthplace
  of the world
mom didn't care if the sea swallowed her
i thought my mother might turn into a mermaid
  and leave
she swam so fast
deeper and deeper and deeper, dolphins came
it was my grandmother, we all knew it
she was diving with us, her promise to never leave
when i am lost, i find the sea, and that's where
  she finds me

a love like mine might scare you

i won't try and push you away
if you leave, it's okay
being emotional should not be a deal-breaker
   feeling everything, feeling the world
is not something i am able to hide
if you stay by my side
me, *wild with sensitivity*,
and choose to love this whole moon-admiring,
star-firing thing,
i may start to cling, but i will always give space as well
if i get to tell you what lives in my soul when the night
   feels like forever
then, darling, there is nowhere i'd rather be than together

don't feed the fears

there is a shadow in the corner of our love life
we've moved on
some days, i shine a candle, but the shadow is still there
a lump in my throat, uncomfortable
we've moved on, but my insecurity is still staring
we don't talk about the insecurity, we've moved on,
  remember?
insecurity now disguised as silence
the shadow needs more light
we are too afraid to see it, hide the matches
we prefer to keep it in the second bedroom
  with all the storage
we can unpack it later
for now, we focus on the other rooms
  filled with flowers and windows
close the door with the suspicious shadow
that shapes into everything when it is dark
and here becomes the only world i know

chapter three

Dancing Humans

for the ones who lost their shine,
i hope this makes you sparkle

for the love of all things

we are only here to love
why did we complicate our paths?
searching for purpose in other places when the
meaning is right in front of us?
all these people with empty hands,
simple spaces to hold
when will we start to fold?
could we not dance to the soft opening of eyes?
here for a short time
we must love and hold
for the love of all things, please just hold
when did we forget?
when did we choose to close? to be alone?
we must love
let it drag you out of bed, let it force your steps,
let it sweat out from your skin, harvest within
look, there is the meaning
go down screaming
i am here to love

as the moon shifts through cycles, so do we
there is no "perfection" we aim to be
from a crescent curve to a glowing sphere,
each phase is a reflection of you, my dear

fall in love

fall in love with paintings
and swings in parks,
your eyes and their sparks
fall in love with cooking,
stirring tomato soup
loop by loop
fall in love with rain, giggles, and play,
drawing and clay,
the moulding and the holding
fall in love with dancing,
the moon enchanting, light surrounding
as you spin on the floor, i beg of you
fall in love with much, *much* more

the truth about happy

you don't have to be happy, be gorgeously human
this does not mean to look beautiful, looking beautiful
 is fine
it's not necessary (it's not that interesting), it's nice
add some spice: sit on the floor and eat broccoli with
 your hands
write about sloths or clouds when you feel depressed,
 i'll read it
i'll see your human, when people comment on the blue
 under your eyes,
smile and say, "life," 'cause that's all it is
we breathe and die, go on walks, and make friends with
 people we
don't see enough because "time," things go wrong,
 and even when
they go "okay" we get scared because we know what
 can go wrong, and that
in itself is enough not to wake, we anticipate, you don't
 have to be happy
it's not possible, not all the time, be content with the
 sadness and the rage
happy will fade and come in waves, you will be a human
 in all of this
there is no crisis, just exist

all the world's a stage

you never see the same sunset twice
some humans will disappear from sight
how terrifying, i don't know when
there are no clues
there are no cues
this isn't a rehearsal, this life isn't a rehearsal
you learn lines as you go
play yourself until it stops being a role
nothing is known, we have a stage, and then it is gone
enjoy the performance and the applause
the standing ovation will soon be yours

there isn't a winter that lasts forever
spring will show her face again

young together

let's go dancing in the living room
put on a little show
a wonderland of intimacy
dressing purple, *fancy*
how lucky to have fun
i think, maybe,
you're definitely the one

how to get out of bed

remember the stars were up all night
they are still there during the day, but they are hiding
they want to give you space to shine

there is a warm drink only minutes away from
  being made
you can write something about a rabbit
they have long toes and can't vomit

do some stretches and shake your body
make pterodactyl noises
bonus if you have an estranged roommate

go for a walk and try to spot as many flowers as you can
give one of them a name like *Frankie*
make him your friend

now you will have a good day
flower friends and bunny poems
you are a champion at being human

thank the world for love

and water to cover my body as i leap into oceans
thank the world for hands to hold
thank the universe for breath and air and cool wind
thank the voice for music, *turning into dancing honeybees*
we intertwine, thank the wine
for giggles and gorgeous truth
thank the mothers who soothe
thank you, at last i am safe
for you became my favourite place

where you are now is just as sweet
as the anticipation you feel
for tomorrow

moments of magic

the recipe for joy is simply surrounding yourself
  with silly friends
laugh at yourself and laugh with each other
find the ones who match your weirdness
life can be hard, find people who make it better
here we are, living and crying and breathing on a flying
  ball floating through space
we could all use a hug right now

begging to start living

when the world seems too overwhelming,
and i don't think i can carry on,
my body begs me to start living
there hasn't been enough living
of this one life
there is too much guilt that this one life has not
 been right
full potential hanging over like a threat
"are you there yet?"
sick with all the time i have wasted
have i done enough?
there aren't enough drawings in my room
if there aren't enough drawings, what am i doing here?
where are all the colours? should there be more poems?
there will never be enough poems

why the rush? *there will be time*
i will hold on to this one life
of mine

instant sunlight

friends are extremely beautiful
not just in the way they look
but how they care for one another
how they become warriors when someone is low
they reach out their hands
sharing stories of love
they keep secrets
some friendships will always be worth protecting
it is your most precious asset
be there for one another
your friends are beautiful

you have the power to create a beautiful life
each and every moment is an opportunity to add flowers

fleeting comfort

i miss some people who i only met once
in a garden or a celebration, and it felt easy
there are people who i wish to see again,
but i don't know their names
only that they brought comfort
we connected instantly
without knowing a lot about each other (or anything)
a moment, *fleeting*
this is something i miss

the world is new

we can wake up and choose to appreciate this life
we can change our perspective
learn to love breathing
air is a miracle, now add the sky
every time you leave the house,
see it as an exploration
a cloud surprises you with a different shape
dogs jumping like their first time outside
i want to live like that, as if the world is new
and then i remember it's already true

i am you, you are me

treat everyone like a reincarnation of yourself
we all melt and intertwine, infinite by design
don't look down and rush
there are more hearts to touch
good news, this isn't all about you
take the pressure off and become soft
only human is what we seem to be
you forget, we are an entire galaxy

i want

i want to invite people for dinner and have a theme
i want to be extra
i want to play with more pets
i want to overdress
i want to write meaningful letters to friends
i want to find ways to love myself each day
i want to be good alone
i want to feel the calm from deep within
i want to walk next to the sea and pick up shells
i want to sing ABBA in the car
i want to surprise you with a picnic
i want to sit in libraries
i want to be the human version of a hug
i want to hold you a little longer
i want to tell people i appreciate them
i want to be a home for others
i think we can all become safe spaces

parts of me

i am not simply a body,
rather the things i write,
the humans i miss at night,
the water and the storm, chaos and the warm
my love, yes, all the love i give,
the love i receive, this voice, the fears,
ferocious tears,
oh, the desires, oh, the passion,
oh, the oh's
my friends, my beautiful friends,
the things i've called home, the skies, the ocean, its foam,
all that i have seen, my dreams,
this emotion and sway, beg the moon to stay,
the rhymes that run away
i am not yet complete, more of myself to meet
how wonderful to be
and love the parts of me

dancing, dancing humans

i want this life, let us be dancing humans
let us invite more legs to pirouette and step
believe in light even when there's none
inside, you'll find the sun
let life lead, go to the unforeseen
even when it feels like the end, we emerge again
in bright colour, an open heart, new eyes that spark
we dance the days, we find our place,
we stay
allow chaos to lead the way

gaia girl

did you forget how to play with clouds and give
  them names?
i haven't seen you dancing again
there is some mud outside good for baking
draw a picture of a butterfly chasing
yes, catching bugs can be scary, but they
like gardens, and they don't feel little
neither should you
hearts are really big, and yours has a smiley face on it
you're really pretty when you believe in yourself,
and when you give me a massage, i'll give you one too
here is a painting i made for you, animals are so cool
i'll never fear being a fool
i cuddle like a caterpillar, possessed
when we watch a movie, i'll build a nest
i saw a bird do it once, and i'm quite sure i have
  more fingers
don't worry if you lay an egg, we'll take care of it
your wings are still baby small, but when you're friends
  with a cloud,
she won't make you fall

create your beautiful life

you are here
part of the atmosphere
craving hugs like people do
wholesomely human, wholesomely you
a body of art,
blood and heart,
a star, part of everything,
leaving trails, whispering,
smelling flowers, planning the hours
simply breathe, and please
never leave
you look good happy, but you're a masterpiece
  when you try to find,
when you don't want to leave purpose behind,
when you cry
we are all trying to be found,
listening for some insightful sound
look around
you are not alone in this disorder
be an absorber, and create a world that you adore
see, that's a life worth living for

take care of the world

take your frustration
and spread some much-needed light
maybe you are tired of feeling helpless
energy comes from kindness
send it to our world
you don't have to be alone
one soul
we are all here sharing, live by caring
be better, bring the bright
and the fires? *ignite*
little candles walking along
smile at someone
it's not hard to do a small part
leave things more beautiful than you found them
and love will grow, even from within

time to do hard things

we must do things that scare us
comfort zones are cosy traps
where is your spark? can you find it?
pick up the matches, *light it*
kick off your shoes and run towards the deep
dive in, how marvellous, you float!
how strong you swim
who knew arms could reach so damn far?
how long you've held your breath,
and all you needed was to try
all this life under one sky

chapter four

Adore Yourself in Ugliness

slow down, take a deep breath

adore yourself in ugliness

when your legs are smothered in grass burns,
hold your tender body close
let it melt into you, the days you forget how to do
  anything but cry,
as the fogged mirror is swept by your hands
you exist brilliantly, in strawberry-stained sweatpants,
popcorn-smeared dust, and you forget that there is time
adore your mind when you want to think of nothing,
when being is more than good,
as you stare at water, but lifting anything but your head
  is death
adore yourself when you can't take care,
when the shadows are everywhere, lurking deep,
too tired to clean, when you only want to sleep
don't brush your teeth
love the mess, your hair as a nest
look at your red eyes and see the fighter, ravished
  in resilience
adore as you fall to the floor, as you crawl
you are still here, slithering loudly through silence
you are blazing, you are bright
adore the ugly and love the night

body check-in

gift yourself a moment of self-regulation
get back into your body
inhale, hold your breath, and, when you're ready,
breathe out
keep going
notice when you have the urge to rush
when you want to get on to the next moment as quickly
  as possible
that's when you breathe
when your mind jumps ahead
inhale
exhale
do not shame yourself for trying to get on with your day
be with it
be with your thoughts
accept where you are
simply breathe
and feel

seeing people you've lost contact with

i saw you today, but i couldn't say hello
you didn't want to be noticed
just a quick rush to the grocery store
buying basil for a caprese salad
wearing sweatpants with fuzz balls stuck to them
your hair was still wet,
mascara smudged under your eyes
you were tired, but i could see you were very much living
it was good to see you
you looked beautiful in a rush, my busy friend
flustered in the queue
i wanted to greet you, but i knew you wanted
  to be invisible
i want to be left alone some days too
it was good to see you
i miss you

bring her back

my younger self is more wise
i write letters to her in the hope of advice
she'll know what to do
she always comes through
to figure it out

she'll know what this is about
the meaning of breathing
the reason people keep leaving

just have fun
is something she would say
lay the stress to rest

i can't let her down
though it has been hard for each new day to start

it is our duty to see the beauty
in everything
and sing

believe in this world
every day has a pearl

her voice is soft, but i need her to shout
my goodness, i wish to make her proud

this was a hard day

perhaps i am writing because i am anxious
there are so many things on this coffee table
i scan my day as piles unfold
i want someone to hold
i know i should sleep, but there are monsters
  in all the corners
too much busy life, it never ends
it extends
what are you going to do? you can pretend
  to be a baby again
that's nice until you can't because you are the
only one who takes care of yourself, remember?
i remember
please calm this heart
tell her life can be art
life is difficult
now get some rest
put away the cups
you did your best

**on grief
(a home for pain)**

when you don't know what to do with pain,
don't do anything
you don't have to fix it immediately or try and get rid of it
you can simply feel
give space to pain
this space can be pretty uncomfortable,
but it will give you the experience that you need
listen to your body
don't judge your feelings
you may want to run
try and sit with pain
for your feelings are never wrong

self-empathy

for a long time, i was angry about the things
  i didn't accomplish
and annoyed with everything i did wrong
looking back, i understand
i was simply surviving, i didn't know any better
i was doing my best with the knowledge available
  to me at the time
you must look back with love,
look back with empathy, and forgive yourself
  for being harsh
everyone is simply doing their best

the human experience

you can try and hide away from pain in this life
in time you will see,
difficult things carry more meaning than you think
you will see that growth often means to let go,
and patience has a way of healing the soul
the human experience is filled with struggles,
but it is also filled with love
do not rush through moments of meaning
sit through the wind and the hail and the rain
the moon will come and talk about pain
there is both light and darkness ahead
you will move forward despite being scared

you can be proud

if no one told you this recently, *you can be proud*
there doesn't have to be a big and recent accomplishment
you've come a long way, despite countless
  disappointments,
and no one knows what you've been through,
  it's only you,
and you've handled everything life's thrown
  in your direction
you fought to make it here without knowing how hard
  it would be,
and you will always make it as long as you keep
  trusting yourself
be proud and keep moving forward with kindness and
  appreciation

fairies don't have everything figured out

you don't have to be a person today
you don't have to be put together if you're not okay
take a moment
and feel what you need
be a flower or tiny seed
sit in your soil, have some air
drink your water with tender care
you can be a person tomorrow or next week
create a powerpoint and wash your feet
for now, you are a nervous fairy
because adulting
is pretty scary

i am not as strong as i look

the sensitive one, yes
don't pull my hair for a test
and most definitely *do not break my heart*
don't make me fall apart
and don't say "don't"
i am very involved with emotions
i put the "path" in "empath" because you can trust i'll
follow your feelings too
becoming you
don't be angry with me
i know you didn't scream
it feels that way
now promise you'll stay
my mind becomes blank
i freeze
i can't do conflict,
not when you're mad
i'm never angry, only sad
leave me to write it away
through this, i'll think of something to say

you cannot tell me you are not beautiful

you cannot point at flaws on your body
  and call them ugly
we were taught to shame ourselves
to find faults, from the length of our lashes to the
  chipping acrylic on our toes
compare fancy clothes or a perfect nose
you are beautiful just as you are
you cannot tell me you are not
as you make eyes spark and friends laugh around
  the dinner table
pretty is just a label
i prefer a heart of gold and friends who hold,
people who listen and share, have empathy and care
that's a lot more important than what i can see
now you know,
you are the most beautiful to me

i don't know who needs to hear this today, but . . .

you are not a failure
no one compares you to other people the way you
  compare yourself
no one sees your imperfections with your critical eye
you are so much more than your body, your job,
  and your accomplishments
treat yourself with the love you give away so freely
thank your heart for beating
life is more beautiful when you see the magic within
now get up and, without judgement, begin

a place of rest

explain to me
simplicity
the things worth remembering
as my mind morphs to a mouldy mess, wild with worry,
i tell myself a story
and obsess with stress,
but somewhere on a mountain lives a place of rest,
creating breath
let the river in
rub honey on your skin
wait for a pink-purple sky at dawn
adore the truth and be reborn

i don't think there's anything special about me,
just a walking star and a talking heart
what's so special about that?

(winky face)

the walk of life

are you behind?
regret in your mind?
is the bank account leaking, with life speeding?
are you a wife? alone?
do you own a home?
do you go to the gym? is your goal to be slim?
how healthy is your diet?
tell me: *do you know the quiet?*
or do you ache for blasts of sound?
are your friends still around
or did they leave for the seas?
have you met peace? can you sit with subtleties?
do you know any dances? have you taken chances?
do you wish to squish time into life?
you are allowed to take it day by day
everyone has a different way
this is the walk of life, yours is sweet,
utter nonsense to ever compete

i am small

small like a star, small from afar
i am small like my heart
calling poetry art
i am small like the quiet
nowhere but all around
small like a simple sound
saying *i am here*
small, but still
i appear
eyes and mind shifting
a moon forever drifting
though i feel small,
i think
i am not
not small
not small at all

absolutely precious

this time, the walls are crying with you
they don't stare, only wish to hold and fold over you
too precious
don't give up
the moon calls you her sister,
and still
you forget your worth

wish for your life

she imagined her life would be different by now
holding hope to be one of the lucky ones
more in love, more wealthy, more fit with more friends
but when the star travelled across the skies,
she closed her eyes to dream of another life
but couldn't find one with the same mother, pet dog,
best friend, and memories of dancing,
even her own hands and bed were different,
familiar things taken for granted
she realised there is no other life to desire,
for her life is one to admire
no wishing away, we stay,
we stay

a poem for myself

let me hold you
people don't understand your feelings,
but you will always be strong enough to carry on
you weren't prepared for how your soul would respond
it's not your fault for feeling this deeply,
like everything is too much to handle
i will save you every time
this is my vow, *ink on paper*
i promise to hold you in times of loneliness
when i lose you in mornings,
i will find you at night

you are whole now

we call it healing or a place to reach
you are not something to fix
we grow, go slow, struggle to know,
but we are whole
as we dance and grieve,
as people leave
we are allowed to be lost,
afraid of the dust,
scared to simply trust, but we
will always be
whole

look at the whispers

quiet now, you have been good
it's not your fault as pressure wraps around
keep on carrying hope
lie down and float on a downhill slope
other people look impressive,
but they have battles each night
demons feast when out of sight
you'll have your time, slow climb
nudge and touch each stone
you're not alone and never will be
these rocks can fall into the sea, *splashing like stress*
lay them to rest, take in the scene
look, you're further than you've ever been

retreat

my confidence is taking a break
it's not the end of the world
the waves will always turn
the sickle of a moon will grow full

to be small doesn't hurt anyone
stars go into hiding too
i won't fake being okay
it's just a bad day

my clothes fit differently,
and i want a moment to hold my beautiful body
i am allowed to feel a little strange
and with time comes inner change

and how is your anxiety doing?

she is me, i laugh clumsily,
and we are doing all right
we are roommates (more precise)
cannot kick anxiety out
pays rent and my therapist
lets me do the chores, screams at my missteps
i have begged her to leave or find another place
"we learn to live together," she says
staring in eyes and clapping her flat hand on my chest,
ba bump, ba bump, i detest
not sure if anxiety finds it amusing
i find it cruel, i don't love you
we breathe together, and i realise she won't move along
she means well in all her wrong,
saying such sickening things,
attempting to create more hate in my house
she means well, but can i shut her mouth?
i beg anxiety to sit in another room,
not on my lap, please,
not with a grip to smother me,
and then i see and know,
anxiety won't go
this is where she prefers to be
i calm her down, i stroke her gently,
say, "i won't leave,"
for you are me

my soft-sided part

oh dear,
the sad self has appeared,
the one i cannot seem to shake
do not bother asking her to leave
let me be
it doesn't work like that
you cannot get rid of yourself
embrace the imperfections,
less focus on corrections
i cannot go to war with myself
this body is one thing,
one being
therefore, i must forgive this sadness,
an unknowing, melancholy nothingness,
because my soft-sided part
is also sharing my heart

chapter five

You Are Loved/
You Are Love

ordinary love

i look at you pouring the coffee,
a task i have seen you do a hundred times,
and suddenly a whole lifetime
doesn't seem to be nearly enough time

just the two of us

you chop the onions so i don't cry
you call for pizza delivery because i'm shy
you bought me a knitted unicorn, and i cried anyway
you're better with actions than choosing words to say
i try not to, but i always get food on my clothes
you roll your eyes and laugh like *you're happy*
  with the girl you chose
i love being absolutely silly with you
i love laughing and having the zoomies before bed
i can't believe every night i have a sleepover
  with my best friend
life is sweeter when you're next to me
someday i'll chop an onion,
but there's no guarantee

for days filled with tears

step into the sun, my love
tell me
tell me everything that you are feeling
i will be here to listen, *quiet i will stay*
and hold your hand along the way
slow and safe, you have a place
you belong
take a deep breath, step out of the rain
into the sun, slow and safe
a warm place, let go of your breath
all that is left, be with sadness, for you are one
be with sadness
step into the sun

if you love me, tell me
don't let me guess what you are feeling
just say it
kiss my face
i'll say it back
kiss my face

allow yourself the full magnitude of love

i love you, because

you taught me to take the ocean route home
you said, "we should grab on to beautiful things
  when they arrive"
you never rush life, but with you, time always flies
now, instead of looking ahead, i focus on the moment
i don't care if it lingers
i keep the beauty from slipping through my fingers

don't say "i love you"

don't say it because it's part of the motion
every night before bed or when you hang up the phone
just as a reflex
"i love you"
say it because there is an ocean that cannot be tamed,
butterflies screaming,
and the fire of passion cannot be held by dragons
  any longer
i love you because cupid is being strangled,
using broken arrows to untie his wrists,
let me out!
say it because you need to,
as you crave to speak it
there are many things we do habitually
do not let love be one of them
sit with love and unleash it onto me,
and i will match your love
in glorious battle

you are my most important poem

under the sheets, you can press your cold feet
  against my legs
when you forget a towel for the shower,
i will spread and wrap it around like a grand cocoon
you can be big or little spoon,
for you are the most important poem i'll ever write
'tis a gift to roll over and kiss good night
i will love you as much as i know,
and in return, i hope you won't go
after we've shared a thousand sunsets
and a thousand cups of tea
there is no mundane moment that means nothing to me
each detail of our life is pure and exciting
that's why you're the poem i'll never stop writing

love moments of safety

you keep my feet from falling off the sofa, and i become
  a blanket
i've cried like the ocean this week, i can't speak,
but you inspect my tears so tender
this is how i spend december
wet eyed and loved, close to your touch
we walk with small talks
and watch *waves*
i try to freeze days
not being able to pause makes me cry, you're by my side
and don't understand the sad, i show you falling sand,
  say, "i'm cold"
you always hold
"i don't like my body," and you say, "no"
we walk again, you're my best friend
next year, i might cry less,
but there lives a bucket for me on your chest

to the moon and back and to the
moon and back again

call me extreme
if you need water, i'll catch rain and save it in my palms
when you need rest, i'll give you my arms
they'll form a chrysalis for you to be soothed, i'll have
  nightmares removed,
place stardust in my pockets, a path to follow when
  you are lost
when the world is hard, i'll always be soft
when tears fall and you don't want to speak,
i'll catch them as they meet your cheek
no need to talk,
i'll call the birds as we go for a walk,
point at little things i see, like yellow trees, like leaves
  drifting on the breeze
call me extreme, but, my love,
i swear i'll never leave

this is love

he loves me sad on the kitchen floor
he loves me red-eyed, and still he adores
he loves me,
pink hair dye, he loves me with my lips dry

he loves me *even as a worm*
he confirmed
he loves me, sweatpants and a five-step skin care routine
he loves me mean and hungry
(when i am mean, i am usually just hungry)
he loves me, girl dinner and sad songs
he loves me in all my wrongs
most of the time, i apologise
he loves me as wide as the sea
he loves me like poetry, and i love him
uncontrollably

people ask me about the sun, and i only hear your name

arms

i read somewhere that hands grow out from the
  heartspace
in the womb, little arms spring from the heart
when we hug, our hearts hug
it's a quiet connection,
such strength and healing
life can be love,
and i'm not dreaming

hopeless, i tell you

we can watch the moon together, and you can fall asleep
on my shoulder *forever*
this is something i propose
my hair makes a soft pillow, but it tends to scratch
  the nose
you have the most adorable sneeze, so forgive me if there
  is a purposeful prickle
keep your finger away from my belly, i hate that tickle
rather, bat one eyelash next to my jaw
you dream like a cat, and i don't mind if you snore
i like hearing you
i like feeling you
don't make me stop holding
when i feel you unfolding, i pause my breath
i think loving you will be my death

when you are in my life

my door is always open
bring joy or all your sadness
i can boil the kettle and make your favourite drink
in a heartbeat,
prepare something to eat
i have floral pillows on my couch, all trained
  to handle tears
they absorb them with enthusiasm
i can listen
i can speak in life lessons or tell you
i don't know what to say,
but i can stay,
with too many fluffy blankets and sad songs,
and you can stay,
only arrive
we do what we can,
and then we survive

i love you

i love how you treat cats
i love your extensive vocabulary
i love your arms
i love how your lips are always more hydrated than mine
i love your shoulders and the calluses on your hands
i love when we match each other's weirdness
i love when i win
i love watching you drive
i love your freckles
i love how you teach me new things
i love the hair on your chest
i love how you reassure me when i'm overthinking
you are the protector of my solitude
you make me feel seen
not only do you love me
you're also on my team

nicknames and a happy place

pull me in, hold tight
more than that, more than you think
hug me into safety, for a moment,
let's pretend i am thumbelina
you are the flower surrounding me
i'll scribble your name on every page i see
my honey,
you are heaven
i won't make a devil out of you yet
come close, i'll drown in your clothes
obsessed, i guess
obsessed, but yes,
your love is the best
a bit crazy is where the happy sticks
your new pillow
is called my hips

love me like a home

to love someone when things are good
is easy
there is a version of me that is easy to love,
where my hair is shiny,
lips smooth, and summer glows over my soul
anyone can admire perfection
it doesn't make it special
but when the night becomes long
and i forget to hold on,
that's where true love steps in
to love the most unlovable parts,
to love the version covered in marks
and say, no matter what,
your home is my arms

take this poem, for you are home

when the music sounds too loud,
i will turn it down
when you are overwhelmed,
i will make sure you are held
i will dim the light to rest your sight
breathe easy, and believe me,
you can close your eyes
listen as my hands caress your arms
don't worry about your response
you can be still or crying,
but with me,
there's no need for trying

why do i love you?

i seem to remember it was your hands
when we touched, i felt lucky
i felt like a lucky person for the first time
someone who finally had her fears swallowed
  by the ocean
it was your hands
how they held, it felt like they could carry all of me,
not the weight of my body but all of me

be all that you are

you can let the sun hug you today
be sad, i won't tell you not to cry
thank you for being my own personal waterfall
i can't afford a fountain
you can let the moon sing you to sleep
you can weep, i'll tuck your heart into mine
we'll find space, darling
your red face is the most precious planet i've seen
you are my favourite dream
the stars will remember your name
my beautiful disaster, *leave the shame*

i've got you

there isn't an answer to healing
it is a surprise
you scream it out in pillows,
and then you walk alone without music and cry,
and you don't care if people see you
because you are the most beautiful thing they've seen
 in weeks
you are real, and your triggers are valid
you notice them and hold your breath,
but then you miss the air and find your feet,
and when you want to leave, you leave
when you want to speak, you breathe
you move and dance to what makes you feel human
explain this to no one
you don't have time to be misunderstood
the ones who know are the ones who are good

wishes to you

i wish for you more dance in days,
more sun and rays,
more *space*
i wish for you the kiss of trees, the dips in seas,
release
hug the quiet with content
treat the silence as a friend
be gentle in times of storm
chase the ones who keep you warm
you're doing good, stay kind
my wish for you
is to give yourself time

mundane moments of love

our love makes me beautiful
i shimmer in cuddles
we do mini crosswords, and i write poems
  for every part of your face
when i catch an eyelash on your cheek,
  i hope you wish to marry me
you blink and breathe
have you made it yet?
you smile and say,
"yes"

rebel heart

the thing that scares me the most
is love, all this love boiling,
begging to lunge out and become a part of you
where do i place this recklessness?
my heart is an irresponsible rebel
she knows what can happen and still
waits impatiently for you to open the door and let her in
full force, don't fear the flood
i can't keep my heart inside
please accept what stumbles out
it's messy and all over the place,
yet it's beautiful
the terrifying can be terrific
therefore, i will love and be brave
through hesitation and heartbreak horrors
open up and see what happens
this is my love, i hope you like it
this is my love
here, keep it

little bugs

i don't know where to find lasting happiness,
but you seem like a good place to start
at night, i hear you whisper to my heart
will you move in my direction?
only two bugs with one question
are you my person?
the love to keep for all my time lasting?
i am simply asking
as you braid flowers into my hair and walk next
  to the sea as if we have eternity
i wish we had forever, but we have now
i have your mouth
in quiet moments, we find perfection
you're in my mind every second
i've always wanted to feel this
but never dreamed that you exist

the dearest thing i ever spoke

you are my favourite story to tell,
but i can never capture you in poems
only a glimpse, i blink in winks,
one eye at a time to never miss a glance
you've placed me in a trance
don't leave my sight
your taste is daylight,
every single kiss
your body is a miracle or a wish
i forgot i made, perhaps i prayed
somewhere on earth, *you became my universe*
you made me see, now i believe in poetry
words that were lost started to defrost
and woke
your name is the dearest thing i ever spoke

make it obvious

playing hard to get is boring
it's so five years ago
i wouldn't be embarrassed if you paged through
 my journal
and found your name covered in pink hearts 57 times
don't bother repeating how you like your coffee
i know, i remember
i listen to your voice notes more than once
i won't pull silly stunts
or wait days to text back
i'll always pack your favourite snack
you are my favourite snack for all our trips
when you make my heart do funky flips,
i won't make you doubt
you see, that's what love's all about

where you go, there i am

i can travel beyond the sun
and then some more
travel beyond the space to explore
i want to spill and be too much
reaching past the point of touch
with every hold and taste,
i love your face,
and in your eyes is where i'll stay,
for every sunrise here is on display
how could i ever go away?

something worth trying for

i don't mind using all my stars to wish for you
i don't mind living fast as long as i come home
  to your arms
love should be slow
in a world where people are taught to breathe again,
where anxiety lives, smothering,
love has saved me
it also led me close to the end,
where my heart forgot its name,
but love is always worth trying
one more time, again

my darling, you made a poet fall in love with you
now you are going to live forever

my love language is:

taking a picture when i am not looking,
and, after a bad day, you say, "I'm cooking"
it's seeing you write my name on a letter,
holding hands, and drawing together
my love language is a surprise sunset walk
and you seeing when i might need to talk
it's giving me extra ginger from your sushi plate
and pretending that this is our very first date
it's a text that says *you're thinking of me*,
holding a towel as i leave the sea
it's visiting my parents when i'm away,
and asking details about my day
it's playing a song you know i like
or planning a long, impulsive hike
it's getting to know me as if the world were new,
and, in return, i won't ever stop loving you

you look a lot like love

love looks like my eyes when i can't believe
  you're sitting next to me
we drive for hours, and my leg gets more attention
  than the steering wheel
creating shivers, and i like the feel
my goose bumps look a lot like love, how eager
  they are to raise their arms
and reach for your touch

love is your kindness hugging me
we're not anywhere we don't want to be
our love looks like a bright coral sea
as we breathe simplicity
love looks more beautiful together than apart
love looks like it's an absolute pleasure
to give you my heart

Your Scribbles

Your Scribbles

Your Scribbles

Your Scribbles

Your Scribbles

Your Scribbles

Christi Steyn was born in South Africa, where she studied English, theater, and education. She is an avid lover of the ocean, impulsive dance sessions, and conversations with the mountains. Having amassed millions of followers worldwide for her captivating readings of poetry, Christi hopes to make her readers fall in love with words. She believes in adventure and the beauty of storytelling, and she hopes to continue to connect with readers through poetry.

Instagram: christi.steyn
TikTok: christi.steyn.poetry